How to create
Explainer Videos

in PowerPoint 365 und 2019

Ina Koys

Short & Spicy, vol. 6

Contents

0   What we're going to cover

Normally, PowerPoint is used for business presentations, meant to look uniform and business-like. To get this done, certain standard techniques are used which we will IGNORE here.

We'll be looking at a sub-area that sometimes is regarded as a secret science and charged accordingly: the creation of videos. To get this done, we don't need any extra equipment or software, only a computer with PowerPoint installed. One may use microphone or webcam but doesn't need to.

All screenshots are done using PowerPoint 365 but are very similar in PowerPoint 2019 and previous versions. If there are functional differences, I'll point them out.

Mostly, the techniques will explain themselves while actively checking them out. But if you like, you'll get the files used in this booklet clicking

www.ShortAndSpicy.online

Have fun creating your new explainer videos!

1 General settings

In this booklet, we are going to work with initially empty slides. In companies, they are welcome to contain a logo or a footer. But the otherwise really useful content placeholders would only interfere with our examples. That's why we're going to work without them.

Once PowerPoint has opened, you'll normally presented with an empty title slide. Click it and select from the **Layout** choice the **Blank** layout or an empty custom one.

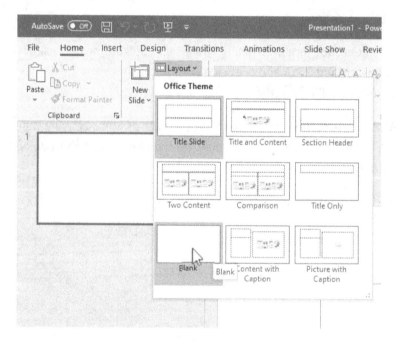

After that, the placeholders are gone, and we have room to work with. To get new slides, click **New Slide** or press **STRG + M.** From now on and in this presentation, you'll always get at first empty slides. To change that, you can change it as you did with the first slide.

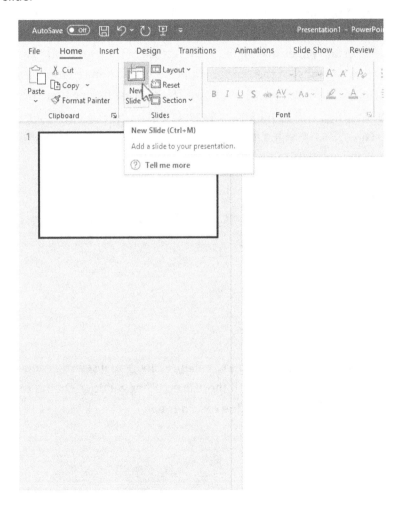

2 Simple screen recordings

Sometimes, you my only want to explain certain steps on the screen to new users. Where to press which buttons or how to find and how to use certain pages in your intranet. In such cases a little video how it's done will most of the times be much quicker than to write, read and follow step-by-step instructions. This process can be done on your machine and simultaneously recorded by PowerPoint. Then, you can store the video in an appropriate place so users can view it again and again as required.

The button is on the right in the **Insert** tab.

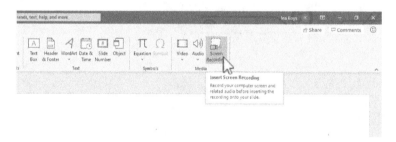

Clicking it, PowerPoint seems to collapse, and you'll see the window just below or your desktop, if there is no other window. On the top of the screen, you now see the recorder bar.

Here we see that the mouse pointer is recorded by default and likewise the sound. You can switch that off if you like. But to start the recording, we first have to specify the respective area of the screen. The recording of the whole screen is possible, but seldom necessary. It produces large files and on small screens (mobiles!) one may not be able to figure out a thing anymore. Therefore, less can be more. Hover the desired screen area with your left mouse button pressed. It is now bordered with a red dotted line.

You may want to test the planned steps beforehand to see whether the frame fits. If not, simply click **Select Area** again and correct your selection. But only after selecting an area the **Record** button will be active. Once you click it, the bar will disappear, and a little countdown starts before the record starts indeed. Now do what you intend to show. If you're finished, move you mouse pointer to the top of the screen so the record bar will be displayed again, and you can stop the record pressing the **Stop** square. The record is now stored in the **Play** arrow. If it's not displayed, you may have to click the video first.

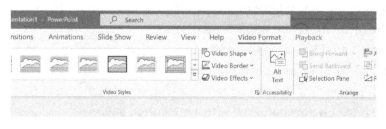

If you're happy with the result, you can store the video in any de-sired storage. To get it done, hover the video with your mouse and press the **RIGHT** mouse button.

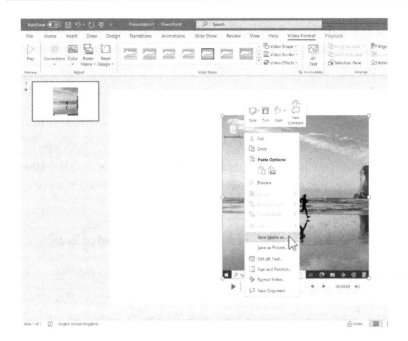

The **Save As** dialogue will open so you can pick a folder of your choice.

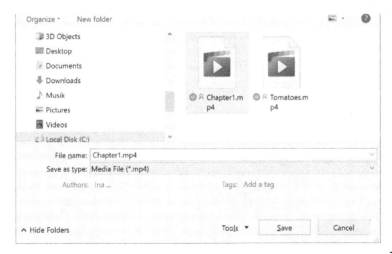

Only one data type is available, *.mp4. But this one is compatible with almost any device. Maybe except really old operating systems and special security settings. But Android and Apple will display it as well as all common browsers. Just in case you want to upload it to a website.

You now saw why I called the chapter 'Simple screen recordings'. One hardly can make it any easier. In the created file also the sound of my voice is included as it was done on the laptop and the microphone was not disabled.

Three tips, before we proceed to more sophisticated projects:

If the upper part of your screen is going to be part of the recorded area, you may dislike the record bar chiming in. In that case, you can alternatively stop the record pressing **Win** + **Shift** + **Q**. The bar will not appear, then.

If you intend to shorten the video at the beginning or end, see you again in the videos chapter.

Watch out for the display of the slides in the PowerPoint window. If anything in the slide is moving – what and how ever – a little star is shown next the slide. It provides better overview.

3 PowerPoint Elements

Only a few explainer videos are as easy to create as a screen record-ing. Most of the times, one wants to combine several images along with written text or spoken narration and of course change the scenes sometimes. All this can first be created in a normal presenta-tion that later can be animated – but doesn't need to. The effects are similar for most of the elements, that's why we'll look at them in chapter 4. First, we'll look at the different elements and some of the special possibilities they provide. If desired, you can use the tech-niques shown also for the elements we are not going to cover here like SmartArts and tables.

3.1 Pictures, icons, and shapes

A picture is worth a thousand words. Therefore, use visualizations whenever possible. If you can, use your own works or pictures with clear copyrights. You can copy images from any website in the net, but that does not mean it's legal! So, if you don't have a legal, ap-propriate picture within reach, you may want to check out sites like

> pixabay.com,
> www.pexels.com,
> www.unsplash.com

or others. But you may reach your goal faster and more structured checking out the suggestions provided by PowerPoint. Also here, you'll stay on the safe side.

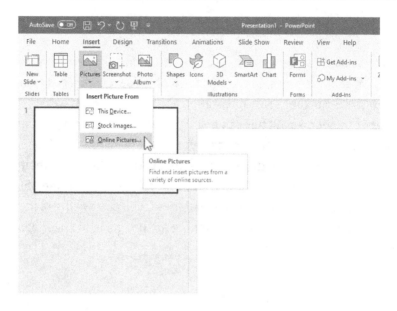

You'll be provided with an extensive thematically structured choice.

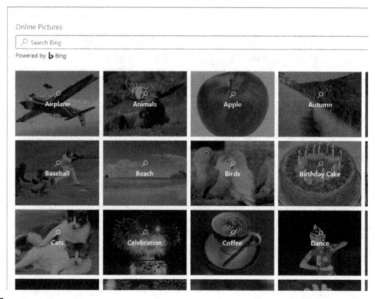

In the input area at the top you can type in search terms and after pressing the **Enter** key you will receive your results.

By default, you will only get pictures uploaded under Creative Commons license, so you can use them legally. Doing a double click you have the desired picture in your presentation.

Chances are that below it, you'll get a license notification like here. In order to get rid of it, first click somewhere else and then on the text border, so only the text shape one is active.

Now, hit **DEL** and the text shape is gone.

We cannot show all the possibilities PowerPoint provides to edit pictures. For good photographs you will anyway seldom need them. But maybe you intend to remove the background from an image. To do so, all you need is PowerPoint and some patience, as here, it's done somewhat different than other picture editors would handle it.

Click on the picture you would like to extract and go to the context sensitive tab **Picture Format** (*Picture Tools / Format* in PowerPoint 2019) displayed on the right the button **Remove Background**.

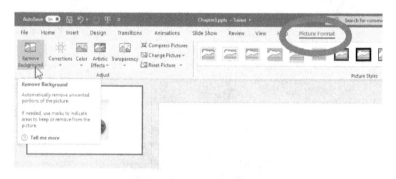

The picture is now displayed with lilac areas. These are the areas PowerPoint intends to hide on the slide. In the ribbon you now find options to adjust and correct PowerPoint's decisions. Test them by clicking one function and then click and drag your mouse pointer across the picture. Sometimes, you will find the reactions funny, but

never mind. Just keep going. One by one, PowerPoint will under-
stand what you mean. And if not or if you made mistakes, relax.
Nothing is going to get deleted. If you're not happy with the outcome, hit **Discard All Changes** and begin anew. Even if you hit **Keep
Changes**, the now invisible parts are invisibly kept in the background.

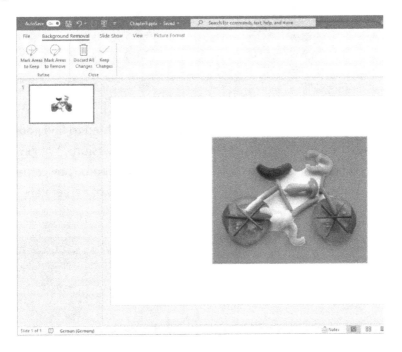

Don't be astonished if the reactions of the app are sometimes a little strange. Under the bonnet, PowerPoint 'thinks' and that doesn't
always deliver the intended results. If you have a special image editing program and are familiar with it and depending on the respective background, it may be quicker to use that one. Anyway:
PowerPoint can deliver a perfectly cut-out motif.

If you prefer icons for your project, you'll be delighted to find good choice provided along with the recent MS Office versions. We get them under the respective button in the **Insert** ribbon. They come with a much more professional look than the ones of earlier versions.

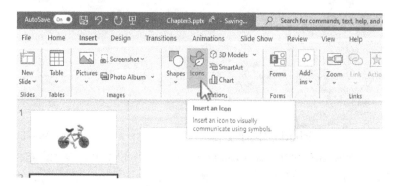

The dialogue opening differs slightly between the versions. Anyway, you'll get a range of categories and a search box. The here also offered tabs **Stock images**, **Cutout people** and **Stickers** are exclusive to PowerPoint 365 and not available in PowerPoint 2019.

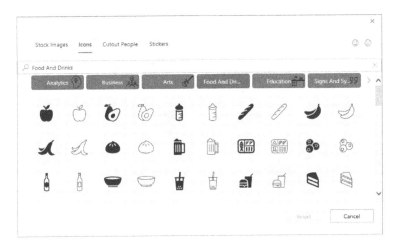

Double-click the burger or any other icon to copy it into a slide. Drag one of its corners to view one of the great advantages of these graphics: you can scale them as you like without losing quality. Also, after clicking one of these icons, you'll get the context-sensitive tab **Graphics Format** (**Graphics Tools** in PowerPoint 2019). Here, you can apply a whole set of changes, i.e. change the colour of an icon.

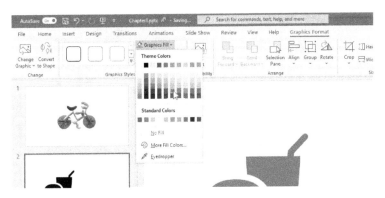

A bit later in this book, we want to mount the burger piece by piece and serve the drink extra. To provide for this, we now disassemble the burger into its parts. To get it done, we click **Convert to Shape**.

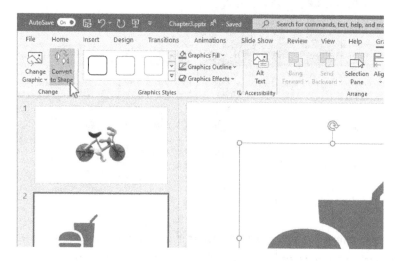

Initially, not much seems to happen. At first glance, everything looks like it did before. Still, a detail has changed: The **Graphic Format** tab disappeared to make room for **Shape Format** (**Drawing Tools** in PowerPoint 2019).

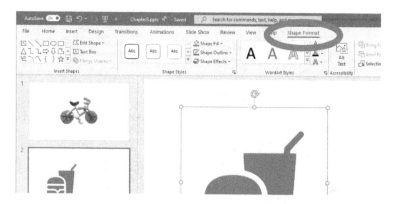

We'll be looking at the standard shapes in a minute, but first, let's stick to our burger meal. It's still highlighted. We wanted to separate and format its pieces which are still grouped. Let's ungroup them.

Every single shape now has a frame of it's own.

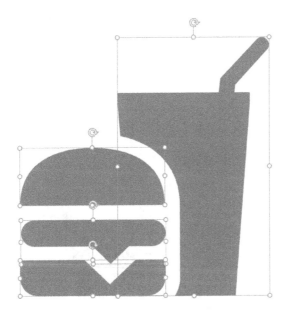

First, click somewhere else and then back on one of the shapes, i.e. the drink. Often, the frame will touch other shapes, too, but most of the times, it will be clear which is which. At least after assigning a

17

different colour any doubt will be gone. I now dye the cup black for the cola it contains.

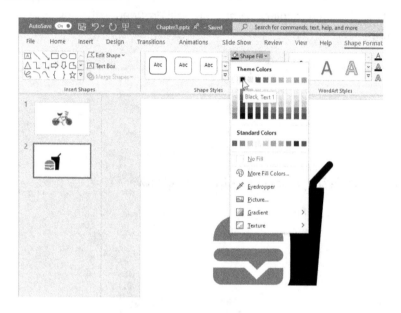

The same way I can colour the two burger buns yellow.

Now, the burger looks nice and for the moment, I leave it this way.

We wanted to have a look at the standard shapes, too. They are around now since a long time and remained pretty unchanged. Sometimes, they may appear a bit fuddy-duddy, but because of their flexibility they will keep their place amongst recommended visualizations for a long time to come.

We are in the **Shapes** tab already. There, we find the choice of shapes on the left. If not there, we find the collection of shapes in many other places like the **Insert** tab together with the other graphic elements.

All these shapes are very flexible and can easily adapted to one's personal taste. I now inserted a **Callout: Left Arrow** into the slide with the burger. We use it to have an example to check out some possibilities shapes can provide. The callout has 8 white dots along its frame when highlighted. I can drag them to change the size. There also is a circle arrow that can be used to turn the shape to any angle. Check that out. Additionally, this callout has like most other elements a bunch of yellow dots adjust proportions, i.e. of the arrow.

Most of the times, the standard proportions are recommendable, but in single cases, they might do well with an adaption. If you did too much one time and would like to go back to standard, the insertion of a new shape will most of the times be quicker than fumbling around with the former one. Still, the options to change the filling or outline colour are in the ribbon **Shape Format (Drawing Tools** in PowerPoint 2019) – we already used them for the burger. Including the different shape effects, you'll find much more than you can sensibly use.

If we now also want to add some text, we have a special shape to get it done: The **Text Box**.

With your left button hold down, drag a frame with your mouse in about the needed size and just write. The text seems to hover over the slide. But indeed, it's in a transparent shape without outline and can be formatted as you like. To change the text display, you don't even need to highlight the text, the active box does together with the **Font** section in the **Home** tab.

These opportunities may open while having a look around on your own. Three other ones are not that obvious.

The first one concerns your settings for shape fill and shape outline. Maybe you'd prefer different ones than initially offered. If so, you can change that for all upcoming ones in this presentation. Format one shape the way you'd like to see all new ones. Then, hover it with your mouse pointer and press the RIGHT mouse button. From the context menu, now select **Set as Default Shape**.

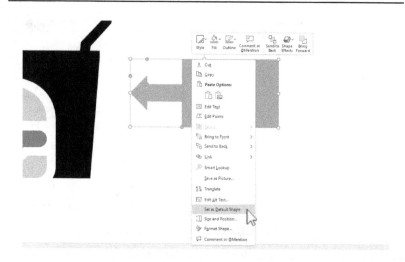

From now on, all new shapes in this presentation will look like this one. And of course, you can still apply individual changes!

The other sometimes undiscovered option is the possibility to insert text in most of the shapes. Just click one – here the callout – and type.

After highlighting it, also this text can be formatted as you like.

And finally, there is a really convenient feature to line up elements. Just move the callout around on your slide. Time and time again, you will get orange dotted lines offering the alignment with other elements. Keep an eye on them! Working with these lines, your work my speed up a lot still looking neat and professional.

Our fast food meal

That's what we ordered!

3.2   Drawings

Drawings are a special element that by default is only offered to the users of touch screens. Others are free to display the tab, too, right-clicking any tab title, left-clicking **Customize the Ribbon...** and then selecting **Draw**. But after that, they would have to write or draw using the mouse on the desk. The result often will be of limited beauty. Apart from that, a good handwriting and / or drawing talent is strongly recommended. But if they are available, you can do visualizations of stunning vividness and with a personal touch. In my case, both talents are tightly limited and therefore will backfire on the beauty of the slide.

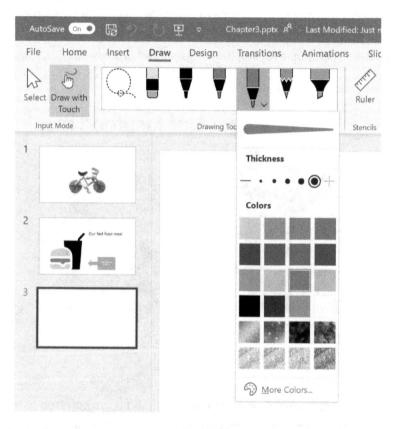

The drawing features of PowerPoint 365 (above) and PowerPoint 2019 slightly differ, still working basically the same. If I want to draw with the finger on the screen, I first must activate the respective feature. With a suitable pen, it's not necessary. Apart from that, I can select from a choice of pens, thicknesses, and colours. I opted for a thicker pen for better readability here. Then I can start – somewhere on the slide.

The users of PowerPoint 365 will find something special on the right in the **Draw** tab: **Ink Replay**. Clicking it, the text or drawing will be drawn anew on the slide. But as one can tell by the lack of a little star next the slide symbol, at this point in a presentation, it will be displayed motionless. We'll care for that later.

3.3 3D-Models

These models are a completely new concept in the recent MS Office versions. At this point, they are rather usable for school education than practical use in companies. Still, if there are own digital models, they of course can be used. We find the 3D models in the **Insert** tab.

The offer is ample indeed and structured – in the upper field one also can conduct a search.

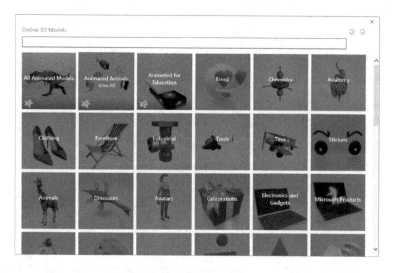

I typed food into the search field and as a result, I received a pepper amongst others. I double-clicked the pepper to download it. The process takes a while as the model is a pretty large file. But as you will see: the models are worth waiting for them!

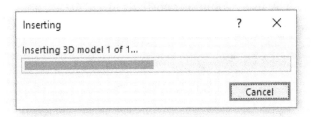

After that, I have the pepper for good and using the symbol in the centre of it, I can twist and turn it as I like. If I want to lay it on the side, like with graphics, I can use the turning arrow on the frame.

And of course, using common shortcuts like **STRG + C** and **STRG + V** I can paste and copy it.

For now, this model does not move at all. But there is a choice of animated 3D models you will get clicking **All Animated Models**. They'll be moving in a in a continuous loop.

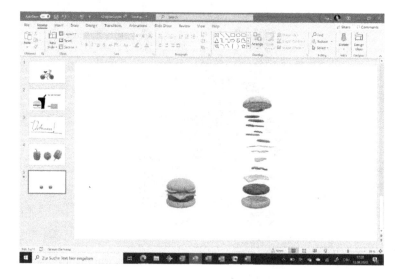

3.4 Videos

As our intention is to create a video, it's somewhat dubious to play another video within it. Still, for the sake of completeness, let's have a look how to insert and trim it. Generally, you can use your own and online videos from different sources. But keep in mind that online videos also come with copyrights and on the other side, remain online. If worse comes worst, they may not be available when you need them. That will only be bad luck for you.

Simply to have an example to play with, I did a short video of the tomatoes on my balcony. It is no piece of arts but does to show the functionality. Find the button in the **Insert** tab on the right.

Even simple videos done with the smartphone are large enough to be displayed all over the slide. Under the video a control stripe is displayed to start and stop the video and to report how long the video was so far. In a presentation, use the arrow in front to start the video. Thus, it's possible to start with some introductory words before the film starts.

If you want to start the video instantly when the slide is displayed, you can go to the context sensitive tab Playback and arrange that.

In this tab you also find the Editing area with the opportunity to trim a video in case you don't want to use some sequences at the end or beginning. To do so, click **Trim Video**.

After that, only the selected part between the green and red mark is getting displayed. Still, the video is kept in full length until you go in the PowerPoint window to *File / Info / Compress Media* to cut off the ends for good.

3.5   Diagrams

Diagrams are the tool of choice to visualize numerical ratio at a glance. Whole books are written on how to design them for maximum impact. Here, we stick to a rather simple display of the recommendations of the German Society for Nutrition.

Clicking the **Chart** icon in the **Insert** tab a dialogue opens with a whole lot of different options and visualizations. Keep in mind that the simpler the look, the easier the message is understood! This is all that counts. For many purposes including ours, the **Clustered columns** are a suitable concept.

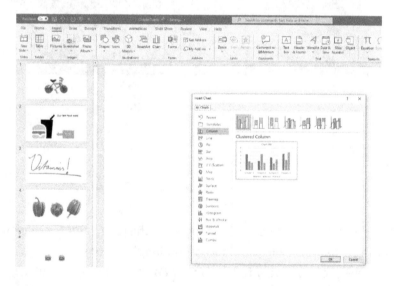

Double-clicking **Clustered Columns,** a chart is inserted in the slide that already comes with some example data. Also, an Excel-like window is opened to change the data as I like. I now type in the above-mentioned nutrition recommendations and can observe the diagram adjusting accordingly.

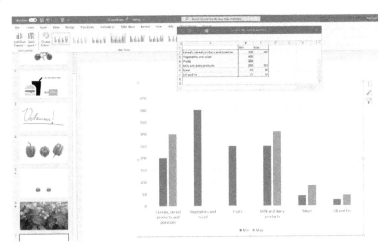

When finished typing, I can simply close the input window. Using the **Plus** symbol on the right of the clicked diagram I now have the **Axis Title** displayed and fill the placeholder with appropriate information.

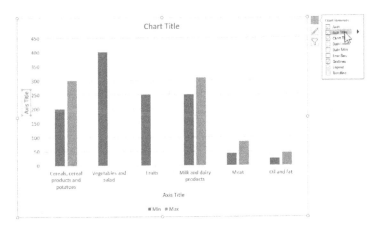

I then deleted the horizontal axis title as I don't need it.

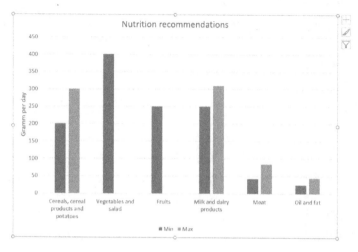

This is all we are going to cover here regarding basic chart functionality. It's only to have an example we can display piece by piece in the next chapter. If really interested in different chart types and options, there is different material to explain it.

3.6   Sounds

In a live presentation given by a person, external sounds have no use. Maybe else if sounds are the core content of the presentation, i.e. if it's about musical instruments.

Here, we're working on a video to be displayed without the narrator being present. In such a context, it might be to silent if not at least subtle background music comes along with it. But also here, do keep in mind, that copyrights apply and you would have to pay for a pop star to accompany your works. If you can't afford that, have your search engine finding royalty-free sounds – you may find them galore. But do read the terms and conditions, they may differ dramatically! For our example, I found a sound that demands a link to the website of origin. That's fine for me, so I can use it.

If I want to get the sound for all the presentation, I have to embed it into the start slide. The button to do so is on the right in the **Insert** tab.

Once the file is embedded into the file, in the middle of the slide a speaker symbol is displayed – also during the presentation. To change that, a click **Play in Background**.

If you additionally or alternatively would like to add i.e. the voice of a narrator, you can use an existing file or record the sound in the spot.

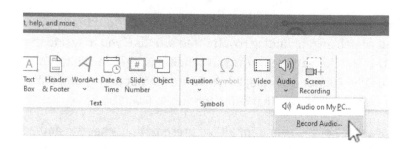

In the window opening you can specify a suitable name, still it doesn't have much significance.

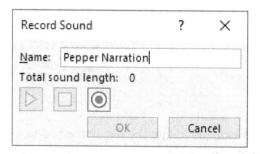

After that, the sound file lives in the slide, still with the speaker symbol to be clicked in order to start. Also this can be fixed. If the **Playback** tab is hidden, click the speaker symbol in your slide. Then, activate **Hide during Show** and from the **Start** dropdown, select **Automatically**.

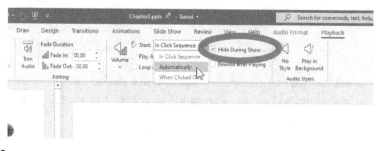

If you now start the show i.e. from the **Slide Show** tab the current slide is displayed along with the sound without any other human interaction.

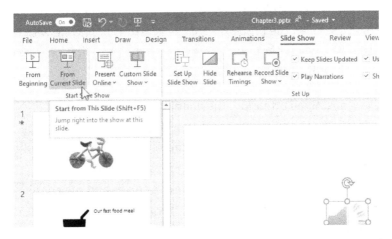

Please note that the background music you may have built in won't be considered this way. It's to be started with the first slide – we are beginning the show from the current slide now.

If starting from the first slide, you will get the background sound throughout the presentation, also if it contents additional sound files like the narration. It is hard to imagine a case when both sounds will make sense together. Therefore, make your decision for one or the other, not for both. I now delete my narration by clicking the speaker symbol and hitting the **DEL** key.

4 Animations

The intention is to create a video. Therefore, the static elements we have so far would look a little strange. From the early years of PowerPoint, we know the pretty meaningless results of playing with the possibilities, when items were thrown into the presentation with triple somersault.

Seeking sustained attention, the animation must be organic. It needs to suit the topic to the audience and the presenter as well. For children, we can certainly use more effects than for the auditors of a company. When doing trainings for bank auditors, I was informed that animations were totally out of place and they don't want to learn anything about them. They quickly changed their minds when I showed them what I call an appropriate business animation. Given that, maybe not all the possibilities explained here will meet your taste. But we're here to examine general options to enable you to make a meaningful selection.

When doing your video, you may sometimes be unsure whether an effect is suitable or not. If so, drop it. Sometimes, less is more. Do keep in mind that no brain is capable of multitasking. People can only concentrate on one thing, anything more is a distractor or does not require any thinking. Utilize animations first of all to channel the attention of your audience to the important point. Only after everything concerning it is shown and explained, proceed to the next one. You are driving a train of thought to a desired recognition, so do it carefully!

Enough words, let's begin now!

4.1   Slide transitions

In a presentation with live audience and a live presenter transitions from one slide to the next are sometimes a bit debatable. They often appear too playful and indeed, don't offer much additional benefit.

But here, we want to create a video that may have to make do without any presenter. In such a case, one may consider slide transitions to visualize some kind of chapter structure.

To check it out, I copied the presentation done in the last chapter, cut out redundant 3D models and take it as starting point for this chapter.

Slide transitions are in the **Transitions** tab.

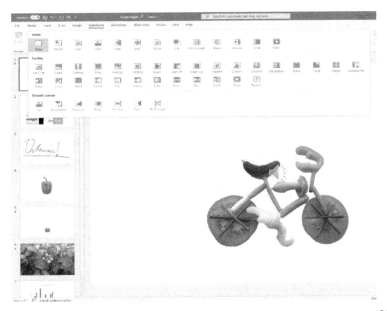

By default, the slides come without transitions. If you click any of the choice of transitions provided, the respective one will be applied to the currently active slide. There is an ample supply of different transitions, but only few of them will make sense for your project. Test them out to get an overview. If you're looking for a transition effect that is suitable for your whole presentation, you will most likely find one in the **Subtle** group on the top. Please note that each of the effects is applied to the fading in of the slide. Depending on the effect, you often get options to adjust it. Sometimes, these options will make the difference between mediocre and spot-on.

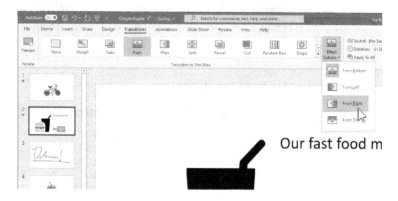

Right of the options, there is also the possibility to adjust the speed of the transition. Make your decision and then click **Apply to All** to make sure the presentation and later the video will be consistent.

Still, we don't want to make it too uniform. Because in some moments you will want to point out the highlights: Achievements of which one is particularly proud of, or problems that eventually are finally solved. Such cases justify the application of a special effect. Just one single time. Otherwise, the effect will wear off and pretty likely only annoy the audience. In our example, I take it as an opener. I therefore add a new slide, this time with **Title Slide** layout as I want a placeholder for the presentation title. I put the title and then change the background colour using the **Design** tab i.e. to dark green.

The title text is hardly readable now, so I highlight it and format the text larger, bold and with white font colour. I also shift the audio file to this new start slide. The second placeholder can be deleted.

Done with that I now go back to the **Transitions** tab and select the now second slide with the veggie bike. I want to provide a little thrill for the audience right at the beginning and therefore, specify the transition **Curtains** exclusively for this slide.

If your presentation is not meant to be too serious, this could be a neat start.

One of the transitions does not explain itself, the Morph. To use it the way it's meant for, we need to prepare some slides. It's because the transition only affects certain objects like shapes, graphics, or title placeholder in a slide. I therefore copy slide 2 with the veggie bike. To do so, I click it, press **CTRL + C**, the put the pointer between slide 2 and 3 and then press **CTRL + V**. Now I have a copy of the slide. That's important, as the effect we're going to apply only works with really <u>the same objects</u> on different slides – not just any looking the same! In the new slide I now i.e. enlarge the bike and put it on its back wheel.

Animations

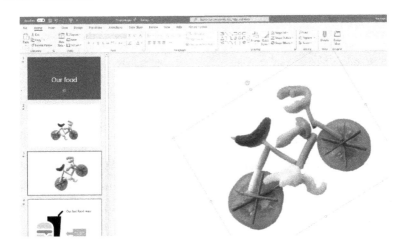

Starting from this new slide 3 that still has the **Curtains** transition in-
herited from slide 2, I now apply the **Morph** transition, only for this
single slide.

The effect is instantly displayed for one time. If you want to check
the presentation from the beginning, activate the title slide and
then i.e. click the little **Slide Show** symbol in the bottom right corner
of the PowerPoint window.

The presentation now starts from the beginning and you can review your works done so far. Each mouse click takes you to the next slide. Hitting **ESC** will end the show and takes you back to the editor window.

Waiting for mouse clicks is a good idea in a normal presentation with a person narrating and explaining. But our aim is to create a video. A video can't be clicked it's just played and might be paused as a max. Therefore, you can specify times how long each single slide will be displayed. If you fix your decisions too early, you may have to do it multiple times again. For the first three slides I don't want to apply changes anymore and therefore can fix the time after which to display the next one.

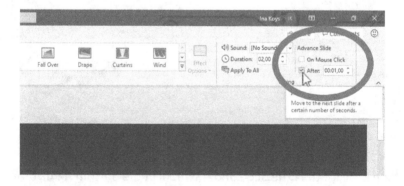

I picked 1 second for these three slides done so far.

But let's return to the morph transition. It is not limited to seamless moves of a picture. We also could do it a different, traditional, way. The morph can – as the name suggests – also change texts and shapes. To have an example, now copy the slide with the burger and the cola and change the text in the text box. Then, click the callout and go to **Shape Format** (**Drawing Tools** in PowerPoint 2019). There, you find in the left upper part the **Edit Shape** feature. Select one that works with text content, I go for the **Cloud**.

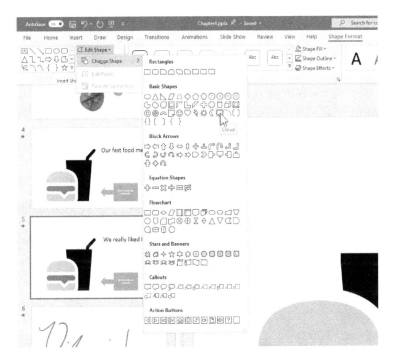

The callout now transforms to a cloud. From the point of Power-Point, it is still the absolute same object. Change more of its properties like colour, font size or text content.

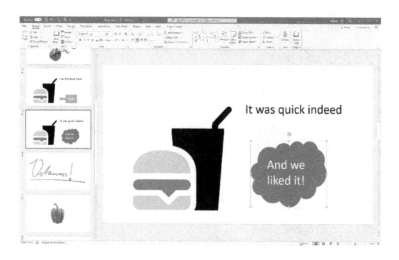

Now apply the **Morph** transition also to this slide. Clicking the **Preview** button, you can watch the text and shape transforming. Maybe you like it already. But do have a look at the options of the **Morph** transition and check whether you would prefer different settings.

If you're happy with the outcome, we now have maxed out the possibilities of the transitions. Maybe, for a serious explainer video, it's already too much. But as mentioned before, our aim is to test and verify the options. Now, let's proceed to the animation of single objects.

4.2   Entrance effects

First of all, entrance effects are used to display the elements of a slide one after the other. Thus, the attention of the audience is focussed on one specific object, not just somewhere. This object would be introduced, explained, and discussed. Only after that, the next one would appear. Nobody would be distracted by irrelevant items. Therefore, the entrance effects are the most widely used animation in PowerPoint by far.

All objects presented here can in principle be assigned the same entrance effects. Whether you assign the effect to a graphic, shape, a text box, or a video – PowerPoint won't care and leave it to your taste. So, let's take the first slide with the burger and the cola now. We disassembled the icon in the last chapter and now want to mount it again, piece by piece.

Generally, it's always a good idea to edit the elements in the same sequence you'd like to display them on the slide. It can later be changed but may result in extra work. In our case, I want to see the text box all the time. Then, I'd like to pile up the burger, serve the drink and in the end add the callout. I therefore first activate the bottom burger bun and go to the **Animations** tab.

In the **Animations** tab we see an array of green stars in the left part. Green stars are all entrance effects. We have a good choice so you can take your time to check them all out. For my burger bun, I will anyway opt for the **Fly In**. But it flies in from bottom, which does not make much sense here. But as soon as I assigned an effect, I will have **Options** activated – at least, most of the times. That differs depending on effect you are examining. For the **Fly In** I can select from 8 different directions. I opt for **From Top** as this gets close to normal work procedures. If required, I also can change the speed of the animation, but feel, the standard is suitable here. After any change of settings, the animation is previewed to facilitate my decisions. Once it's finished, I see a little number next the object. It tells me the number of mouse clicks needed to play the effect in a presentation.

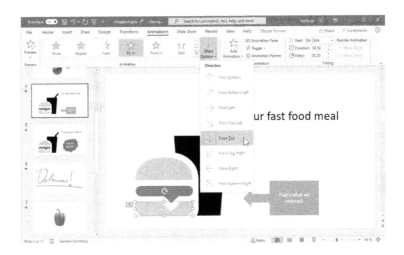

ur fast food meal

Now activate the other parts of the burger and pile them up one by one. After that, you should see three little numbers next the burger parts and can use the **Preview** feature on the left of the **Animations** tab. All not yet animated elements are of course on the screen from the beginning.

Our fast food meal

I now fly in the cola from right and the callout could maybe get zoomed in. So far, I like it this way. Still, all the elements are still waiting for the mouse clicks we won't be able to send to a video. Therefore, in the right part of the Animations tab, I order every single element to appear as soon as the previous one did.

Our fast food meal

Now my whole slide builts up on it's own and in the editor view we see little zeros next each element, informing us that no click is neened to start the animation.

Our fast food meal

If I need to correct something, it will be very convenient to have the **Animation Pane** displayed. There I can highlight items and check which element it refers to. If I like, I can change the order by dragging the entries with the mouse pointer.

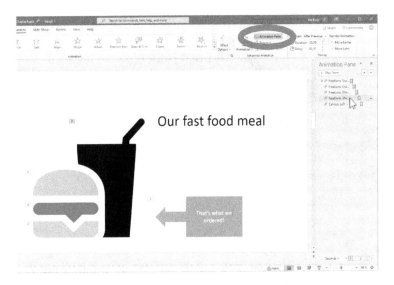

For this slide and as some examples for general entrance effects this should do. The variations suitable for your purposes are something you need to explore and verify yourself anyway.

4.3   Other general effects

Apart from the way how to bring content on the slide, there are also several ways to emphasize elements or remove them from the slide. Do keep in mind that clicking any of the stars in the **Animations** area will overwrite existing settings. To get additional animations, you need to pile them up using the **Add Animation** button.

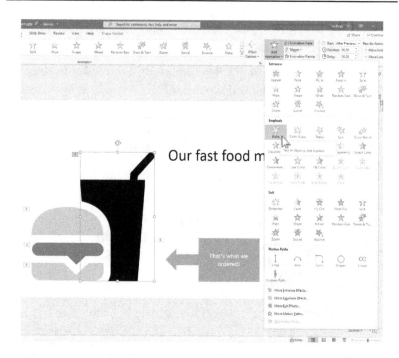

By their nature, entrance- and exit effects can be applied only once per object. Emphasis effects can be applied multiple times. Sometimes, an object may not be suitable for a certain effect, then it will be greyed out. I decided to give the drink a pulse after joining it with the burger. Also this effect initially is played on the mouse click we do not have in the video. I adjust that in the **Animation pane**. There I can again correct the order of effects, i.e. if I prefer to see the pulse after the callout is already there. You also may find it suitable sometimes to start an effect together with a different one. If so, click **Start with Previous**.

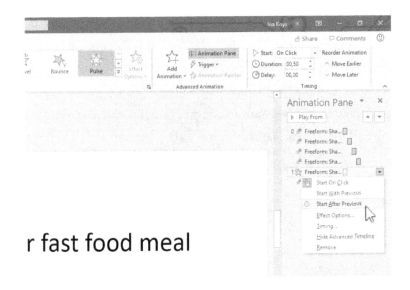

r fast food meal

To move an element across the slide, **Motion Paths** are provided in the **Animations** area below the **Exit** effects. Non-organic moves only applied for the effect itself, are most of the times out of place. Use them with caution. As an example, we may here let the veggie bike drive out of slide 3.

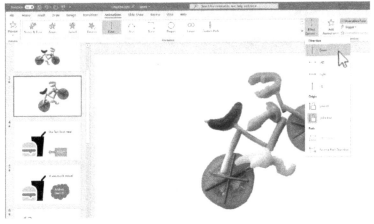

Again, by adapting the effect via the **Effect Options** the result will become more suitable. Alternatively, I can drag the now displayed green and red spots of the animation path with the mouse pointer to define the desired direction and path of the move.

Exit effects are seldom needed as in a new slide an element simply can be left out or deleted. But to have an example we can zoom the cloud out of slide 5.

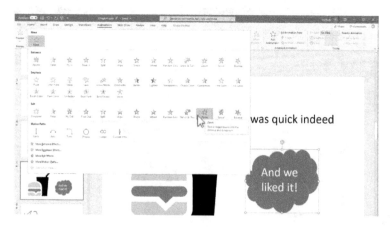

4.4   Special effects

So far, all animations covered can be applied to almost any element of PowerPoint with only slight variations. But several content types have specific opportunities which are sometimes very attractive.

First, let's have a look at the drawing or writing on slide 6. I can have it written anew on the slide.

The effect appears organic and modern and is of course also applicable for drawings. You can start it like any other effect on mouse click, with or after the previous element.

3D Objects like the pepper are well prepared for appropriate animation (and of course, for inappropriate, too). To get it done, they have their own options delivered along with them. I let the pepper arrive and then rotate on a turntable. In the animation pane I made sure, they both are started together.

If you really want to check and adjust all and everything, feel free to apply your changes opening Effect Options. For me it's alright the way it is now. In a real explainer video, you may well display information about the pepper left and right of the object. Whether you do it with text boxes or written text, depends on your style.

Remember: the pepper is in fact a static 3D object. There also are animated ones like the burger on slide 7. These objects come with several different options like different scenes.

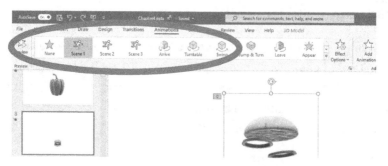

You can make your choice how to assemble the burger. Additionally, to the other animations. To max it out, I now decided to have a bunch of them played one after the other and adjusted start and end timing. The outcome is probably good to attract attention for the moment, but for many purposes certainly already too playful.

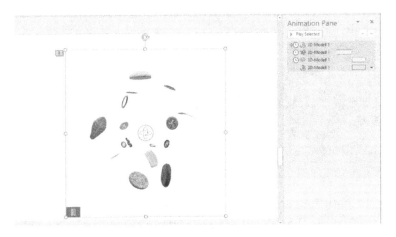

Now let's have a look at the video. In the animation pane we can read that it already has two animations. By mouse click it will start or pause. That's because of the settings we applied when inserting it.

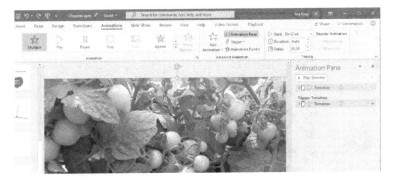

But – you remember that – we cannot send mouse clicks to the final video; it needs to start after previous. I should now adjust that and along with it remove the pause click.

For the basic functions of a video this should be fine so far. But pretty likely, in the video there are comments to leave or moments to explain further. I get the comment done by inserting a text box placed above the video. It could be animated, but I leave it here as is.

Now in a certain moment, I'd like to have an arrow or different shape pointing to a detail maybe explaining it. I can prepare this shape and for a start place it somewhere on top of the video. I then click the video and play it to the moment when the explanation should be displayed. I go to the **Playback** tab and click **Add Bookmark**.

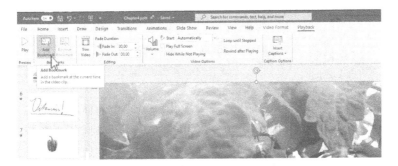

The bookmark is displayed as a yellow dot in the play bar.

Once the video passes this dot, the prepared shape should be displayed. I now position it the way it's meant to appear. Finding the right spot can be a nuisance as the video will always jump back to start when clicking the shape. But using the bookmark we can always quickly get back to the destination and apply better positioning to the shape. Once it's found, the shape gets a simple entrance effect like **Fade**. But I don't want to execute it right now or on mouse click, it's meant to happen when the video passes the book-mark. For purposes like this, we have **Triggers**.

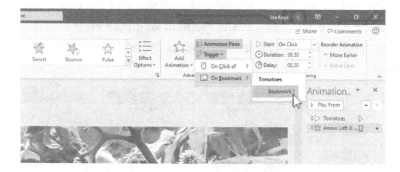

Generally, it's possible to define numerous bookmarks and use them to display, emphasize or hide different objects. Still, the creation of such a construction may lack some fun as there is no possibility to edit existing bookmarks. Neither position nor name or order. If you plan to set up an elaborate cascade of different animations with the video, a screenplay is required. Do create the bookmarks strictly in the right order and the effects accordingly. And if you went into a deadlock, it might be easier to begin from scratch than again to get lost in futile repairs.

Now, one element is left, that almost every time should be animated: Diagrams. In real life, this is not done often enough as many users are not even aware of the possibility. But especially here it is important to focus the attention of the audience to certain values. Otherwise, the density of information in a chart may cause every observer to concentrate on something different not relevant this moment. If we display the data one by one, each of them gets the attention it deserves.

Initially, the effect is disappointing. It's displayed in one piece.

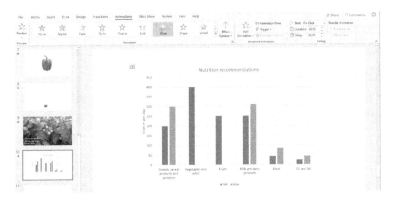

That's the kind of effect nobody needs. Still, don't give up! Fortunately, there are the **Effect Options** which provide meaningful differentiation.

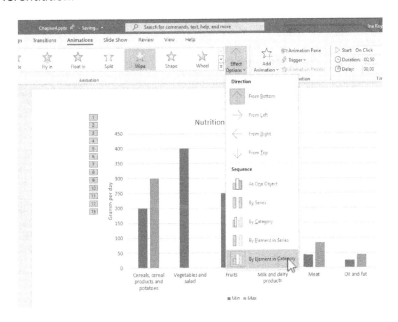

As Element in Category often will be a recommended setting for presentations given by a person. As you see, our example would require 13 mouse clicks to fully unfold. Again, we need to switch them off and therefore, must expand the area using double arrow in the animation pane.

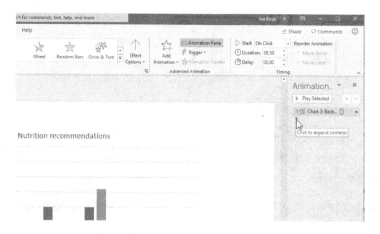

All the chart elements need to be adjusted one by one.

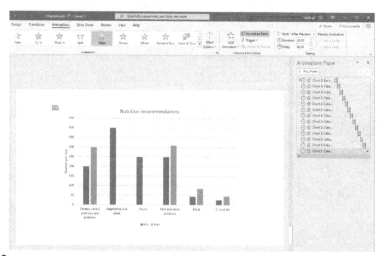

Of course, you can even here apply many more effects. Using the buttons, panes, and technologies we talked of before, I am sure your will find something that suits your purposes.

For the simple reason of room provided in such a small booklet, nothing is mentioned here regarding SmartArts. They are a splendid way of visualization, but their complete variety deserves an own book of this size. I needed to skip them here, therefore. Still, if you are familiar with them, you can animate them pretty much the same as charts.

There is only one element that is not possible to animate with standard procedures: the table. In order to mount them piece by piece or to emphasize parts of it, one really needs to play with tricks. One day, I may also translate my German book about this topic. If you speak German, it's called 'Bewegung!' and available at Amazon, too.

5   Finish and Export

From the content part, our presentation is finished now. But it is still a presentation, no video. Still, the slides 4 to 10 are only shown after mouse click. We had skipped them in before as it was not clear then how long the future animation would take to fully display.

Now, we can take the stopwatch and write the display times on a sheet of paper. Or we can make it easier and have PowerPoint do it for us. In the **Slide Show** tab we find a button called **Rehearse Timing**.

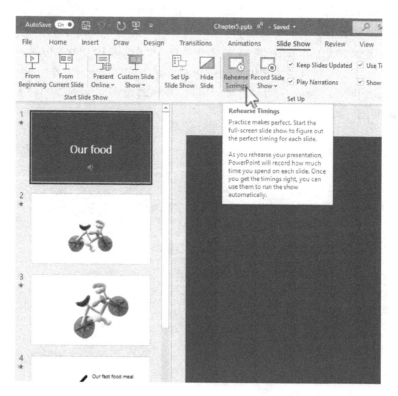

Starting it, I get a little bar to let me advance the presentation once I find the moment suitable.

In the end, I'll get asked whether I want to save the new display times.

If I agree, they will be fixed an I can save the presentation. Still, I remain free to change any timing in the **Transitions** tab on the right.

But it's still a presentation. There are two ways to make it a film strictly speaking or by extension. If I want to divert the file to business workstations, I can assume that each of them has PowerPoint or a compatible application installed. In that case, store the file as **PowerPoint Show (*.ppsx)**.

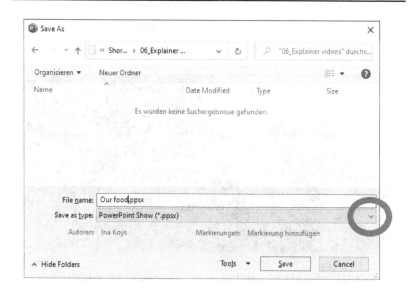

This file type is displayed differently in the Windows Explorer. If you double-click it, the presentation is started instantly without opening the PowerPoint window.

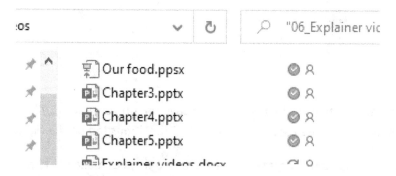

If you still want to edit a *.ppsx file, you need to open it from the PowerPoint window and then can do anything you like. It therefore is something that appears like a video but is none.

If you intend to create a video technically speaking, you find the export function in the backstage area, that is clicking *File / Save a Copy* (or *Save as...*) and unfold the list of file types.

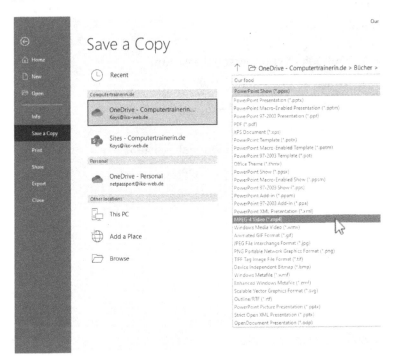

Roughly in the middle, you'll find the **MPEG-4 video**. It's a file type that works on any machine, tablet or smart phone. Conversion and storage may take a while, you can watch it in the status bar.

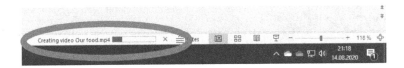

6 More

The **Short & Spicy** series is available for the most part as e-book and print through many distributors. The volumes 1 and 2 are Amazon exclusive.

Vol. 1: Outlook as your personal assistant

Vol. 2: Office 2019 – What's new?

Vol. 3: Office 365 – What's new?

Vol. 4: The Digital Notebook

Vol. 5: Outlook 365 as your personal assistant

Vol. 6: How to create Explainer Videos

Vol. 7: Roll away the boring stuff!

Find these and all new ones clicking
www.shortandspicy.online